The Role of Communication in Large Infrastructure

The Bumbuna Hydroelectric Project in Post-Conflict Sierra Leone

Leonardo Mazzei

Gianmarco Scuppa

THE WORLD BANK
Washington, D.C.

W9-AZZ-744

ISBN-10: 0-8213-6682-3   ISBN-13: 978-0-8213-6682-0
eISBN: 0-8213-6683-1
ISSN: 1726-5878   DOI: 10.1596/978-0-8213-6682-0
Cover art: From the mural in the Bumbuna dam construction camp.

Leonardo Mazzei is a Communications Officer in the Development Communications Division of the External Affairs Department of the World Bank. Gianmarco Scuppa is a Development Communications Specialist in the same division.

Library of Congress Cataloging-in-Publication Data has been requested.

Contents

Abstract

The past decade has witnessed a major shift in the development paradigm, where the increased democratization of the development process is reflected in higher public expectations for participation, transparency, and accountability. In this changing context, the role of communication planning in development projects has significantly broadened. While ensuring that key messages about project design and impacts are widely disseminated and clearly understood remains an important aim, other factors such as building trust, facilitating dialog among all stakeholders, and assessing social and political risks and benefits have come to the forefront in communication processes for development projects. This shift in emphasis is important in today's context to promote more inclusive and informed decisionmaking on the development and management of large infrastructure projects, such as dams. These projects are inherently sensitive and require special attention to the political, social, environmental, and wider development challenges that are linked to successful planning and implementation.

Foreword

One of the poorest countries in the world, Sierra Leone is just coming out of a devastating conflict, with no energy available to sustain its reconstruction, yet with abundant, largely undeveloped, natural resources. With the Bumbuna Hydro Power Project finally coming into operation, the hopes of national recovery are becoming less bleak. Yet this is not enough. Economic growth without concrete opportunities for local community development would represent a missed opportunity, a fact recognized by those working on the Bumbuna project.

Large infrastructure investments and community-level activities represent a continuum of complementary tools whereby one tool builds on the results of the other. Water infrastructure programs can and should be designed to further enhance their impact on poverty alleviation. Local populations, and first among them, project affected communities, should share the benefits of water infrastructure programs. The role of project affected people is central to creating the conditions for development.

Stakeholder participation is a key instrument for identifying and managing risk and uncertainty. Indeed, this is one area where social, economic, and commercial considerations converge. It is in the interest of all concerned parties (governments, developers, lenders, project affected communities, and intended beneficiaries) that issues are resolved early in the project development process.

Increasing evidence indicates that what is usually presented as the "civil society voice" is in reality only a segment of that voice, a segment that legitimately delivers a message about negative impacts of water infrastructure, but remains silent about positive impacts. It is becoming increasingly clear that a better job is required to be more inclusive in engaging "civil society" in options assessment. That job is a difficult one, it requires reaching out to stakeholders who are not vocal, but have a lot to contribute to the quality of projects. In most cases, those stakeholders are not organized to speak with a common voice.

The Bumbuna Team carried out that difficult job in an amazingly efficient and effective way, placing a lot of efforts on grass-roots communication. The present paper describes the approach to, and the implementation of, stakeholder involvement in the completion of the Bumbuna hydropower project. I am particularly proud of the work done by the Project Team and I firmly believe that Bumbuna sets a standard for what we should be doing in similar projects.

Alessandro Palmieri
Lead Dam Specialist
Environment Department, Quality Assurance & Compliance

Acknowledgments

The authors of this case study would like to thank the members of the Bumbuna Hydroelectric Project team for their insightful and meaningful contributions that made this work possible. A special thanks goes to Donal O'Leary, project team leader and firm supporter of the role of communication. A special thanks goes also to Larry Haas and Nigel Wills, exceptional team players who shared their wealth of experiences with great enthusiasm and provided outstanding support and advice. Finally, we would like to thank Paolo Mefalopulos for his valuable inputs, Zita Lichtenberg for her great editorial support, and Johanna Martinson and Caby Verzosa for their assistance and support.

Acronyms and Abbreviations

AfDB	African Development Bank
BHP	Bumbuna Hydroelectric Project
CAP	Communication Action Plan
CBA	Communication-based Assessment
CU	Communication Unit
DevCom	Development Communication Division
EIA	Environmental Impact Assessment
GHG	Green House Gas
GOI	Government of Italy
IEC	Information, Education, and Communication
MDG	Millennium Development Goal
MW	Megawatt
NACSA	National Commission for Social Action
NGO	Non-governmental Organization
NPA	National Power Authority
PAP	Project-affected people
PIU	Project Implementation Unit
RAP	Resettlement Action Plan
SEA	Strategic Environmental Assessment
UN	United Nations
US$	US Dollar
WCD	World Commission on Dams
WB	World Bank

CHAPTER 1

Introduction

Scope of this Paper

Many countries lack the basic physical and social infrastructure that is required to sustain economic growth and deliver essential services to the most vulnerable segments of their population. In this respect, infrastructure development is widely seen as fundamental to strategies to reduce poverty and achieve the Millennium Development Goal (MDG) targets.

In 2003, the World Bank's Water Resource Sector Strategy strongly endorsed the engagement of the World Bank in the development and management of water infrastructure where the Strategy itself broadly characterized essential investment in water infrastructure as "high risk" and "high reward." Because these investments are inherently complex and frequently controversial, particularly in the case of large multi-purpose hydropower projects, the World Bank is constantly exposed to criticism from civil society organizations and international NGOs. Negative campaigns, delays in project preparation and implementation, and even cancellations, have shown that a lack of stakeholder support leads to higher risks and costs.

The past decade has witnessed a broad multi-stakeholder discourse carried out at the international level on the benefits and impacts of infrastructure projects, in particular large dams.[1] Despite continuing disagreements on a number of issues and some fundamentally polarized views, the wider consensus today suggests that decisionmaking around the development and management of large dams should, at minimum:

- use open and transparent options assessment procedures to support strategic decisions on the selection, development, and management of dam and non-dam options;

---

1. This discussion culminated in the establishment of the World Commission on Dams in 1998, a unique example of multistakeholder discussion platform.

- ▓ properly assess all adverse environmental, social, and cultural impacts as an input to final decisions on the implementation of infrastructure projects that are considered;
- ▓ fairly compensate all affected individuals and communities for all their direct and indirect losses caused by the project;
- ▓ beyond compensation provisions, promote longer-term benefit-sharing mechanisms for the communities impacted by or "hosting" the infrastructure project so as to enhance its overall development effectiveness.

and to realize these aims:

- ▓ ensure that there is inclusive and meaningful participation of the involved communities and key water use interests;
- ▓ start this engagement process early, in the upfront steps for project identification and selection, and continue this through all stages of the project cycle where key decisions are made about the development and management of the infrastructure (design and project preparation, construction, operation, and the subsequent rehabilitation/upgrading and decommissioning or re-operation stages).

As the World Commission on Dams report mentioned in its global review of the development effectiveness of large dams, "the most unsatisfactory social outcomes of past dams projects are linked to cases where affected people played no role in the planning process."

In this area, the World Bank has been actively developing and updating its environmental and social safeguard policies that define its support for infrastructure projects. These safeguard policies prescribe the meaningful use of stakeholder consultation and participation mechanisms, which in turn require a skilled and strong communication input if the quality of these engagements is to go beyond a checklist approach. Implementation of the safeguard policies using appropriate management tools provides a platform for stakeholders to interact and work toward a negotiated outcome, for those aspects of the project on which they are empowered to negotiate. Otherwise, it leads to more informed decisions taken over the entire project cycle.

Because this participation must commence at the early stages of project identification and options selection, communication has an important strategic role to play at that stage. For example, Sector Environment Assessments (SEAs), offer an important, relatively new instrument to engage and consult with local populations who would potentially host a project, or be primary beneficiaries. Their effective and early involvement helps to build confidence and community support for any project or initiative that eventually emerges from a decision process. When an infrastructure project is selected, this sets the stage for more constructive multi-stakeholder dialog on the design and operation parameters. Moreover, as the 2003 World Summit on Sustainable Development held in Johannesburg 2003 concluded, partnership approaches are seen as the way forward in developing complex projects in many circumstances, and to maximizing public support and the development effectiveness of these projects.

The World Bank's Water Resource Sector Strategy, argues that an improvement in the quality of stakeholder consultations and participation can reduce the "risk" and increase the

Going the extra mile, visiting the communities in the reservoir area.

"reward" associated with infrastructure projects. It is important to note also that in this set-ting, risk and risk management have expanded definitions. They refer not only to traditional financial, economic and project risks, but also to risks important to all legitimate stake-holders, such as the livelihood risks posed to downstream communities, and risks of non-delivery of essential water and energy services to the beneficiary populations, as well as environment and sustainability risks.

In this changing context, the central role of communication becomes significantly more strategic and broader in scope.

Communication is not only emphasized because of the need to provide new tools and skills to bring a larger number of stakeholders and "decision actors" constructively together to better balance all stakeholder interests, but also because the integrated planning and management approaches that circumscribe infrastructure projects are inherently more complex. In the case of a large hydropower project, for example, the justification for proceeding with the project must be linked to emerging priorities for river basin management and to many other external factors—such as climate change and climatic variability.

Using communication as an analytical tool, and moving it "upstream" in the planning process facilitates timely identification of stakeholders, and allows consultations that enable them to help identify those projects and project parameters most responsive to their needs, building a partnership ethic in responding to their water resource management challenges.

The general principles for improving communication apply equally to the development of new water infrastructure projects and to the renewal of existing projects. This

---

Box 1. History of the Bumbuna Hydroelectric Project

The identification, preparation and implementation of the BHP by the Government of Sierra Leone (GoSL) have been ongoing since 1970.

1970–71: Sierra Leone's first nation-wide hydropower inventory was financed by UNDP. It identified 22 potential sites for hydropower, ranked in order of economic merit. The analysis concluded that the Bumbuna site offered the most attractive option to expand and diversify power supply for the western area grid.

1980: A first comprehensive feasibility study, financed by the World Bank, recommended a 305 MW hydropower project to be developed in five stages. The project design, however, was ambitious and costly. The World Bank considered the project financially risky for Sierra Leone, considering its inability to absorb the generated power capacity, and therefore repay the investment. The World Bank recommended a supplemental feasibility study, which was completed in 1984, and proposed a downsized option that was retained for implementation.

1982: The Government began site preparation works at Bumbuna, involving construction of camps and access roads and excavation of the diversion tunnels on each side of the riverbank. This work was financed by a US$20 million equivalent loan from the Government of Italy (GoI).

1989: The GoI granted a second loan of 138 billion Italian lire and the main civil work started in 1990.

1993: The African Development Bank (AfDB) started cofinancing the project.

1997: The project was due for completion in June 1998. However, disturbances since May 1995 and the eruption of civil war, led in May 1997 to the suspension of the project, when it was nearing completion.

2002: Following the return of peace, the GoSL wished to restart the project and called for the support of the donor community.

2003: In September, a donors' conference gathered the GOI, the AfDB and the World Bank and resulted in a financing plan for the completion of the project.

2004: The completion phase of the project finally started with the implementation of the preparatory studies and the mobilization of the constructor.

2005: In June, the World Bank Board approved an IDA grant of US$12.5 million and an IDA partial risk guarantee of US$38 millions.

paper and case study focus on the latter. Indeed, many of the large dam projects that the World Bank currently supports involve the completion or rehabilitation of existing physical infrastructure.

The 50 MW Bumbuna Hydroelectric Project (BHP) in Sierra Leone discussed in this paper was first identified in the early 1970s. Technical studies to select the site and project parameters spanned the next two decades before the project financing was secured. The main construction works stated in the early 1990s, only to be abandoned in 1997 due to a rebel war, when the project was 85 percent completed. After peace was restored in Sierra Leone, the World Bank responded to the new Government's request to support the completion of the project as a matter of national priority. At that time the Task Team Leader for the BHP authorized the inclusion of a communication component during the project preparation phase. This decision not only proved beneficial to this project, but also demonstrated an understanding of the role of communication in project development that, in the authors' opinion, is all too rare among development professionals.

This paper was written after the Project Appraisal and subsequent approval in June, 2005, by the World Bank Board for support for the project's completion. It aims to demonstrate how a strong and proactive communication component is crucial during the appraisal phases of a project to anticipate and reduce risks and to better reflect stakeholders' interests in project design—thus contributing to fair and efficient project implementation. As discussed in this paper, in the case of the Bumbuna project, a proactive communication component was critical to understand and addressing a number of problems that could have been serious obstacles to smooth completion of the project.

The Context

The Bumbuna Hydroelectric Project

The Bumbuna Hydroelectric Project (BHP) is a multi-phase hydropower complex located on the upper reaches of the Seli River (also called Rokel River) in the Tonkolili District Sierra Leone, approximately 200 km northeast of the city of Freetown.

The objective of the BHP is to provide adequate and reliable energy supply to the western area of Sierra Leone, including the capital, Freetown, to meet current demands at the lowest possible cost, and in a sustainable manner. Development of the BHP is also the cornerstone of the power sector strategy, which is to interconnect provincial towns in the remote northern province and displace high-cost fossil fuel generation based on imported oil.

The main physical aspects of the BHP project consist of:

- an 88 meter-high rock-fill dam with an asphalted concrete upstream face;
- a 50 MW power station located at the toe of the dam, housing two 25 MW turbine-generator units;
- a transmission system consisting of 200 km of 161 kV transmission line from the power station to Freetown and a substation in Freetown to feed power into the western area grid;
- a separate power service to the main towns along the transmission line;

The Bumbuna Dam.

The 30 km reservoir that will form behind the dam will be long and narrow, and have a surface area of 21 square km at the maximum operating level.

The 50 MW project was 85 percent complete when construction works were abandoned in May 1997 due to the conflict raging in the country. In 2004, the project appraisal for the completion of Bumbuna Hydro was initiated with the participation of the World Bank, the African Development Bank and the Government of Italy.

At the time of publishing (April 2006), completion works have already started and the commissioning of the project is expected at the end of 2007.

Post-conflict Sierra Leone

In 2003, when the Government of Sierra Leone called a donors' conference to seek international support for the completion of the Bumbuna Hydropower Project, the situation was not particularly encouraging. Sierra Leone was officially the poorest country in the world, occupying the last position among all countries in both PPP (purchasing power parity), and Gross National Income per capita (World Bank 2005b) on the Human Development Index (UNDP 2005). This was the result of a terrible civil war during which an estimated 150,000 people died (about 3 percent of the population), more than 2 million people (40 percent of the population) were displaced, and atrocities were committed which are still vivid in the memory of the people. The civil war officially ended in January 2002 with the disarming of the last rebel troops by the UN forces. At that time, the UN maintained 17,000 troops in the country, demonstrating that the situation in Sierra Leone was far from stable.

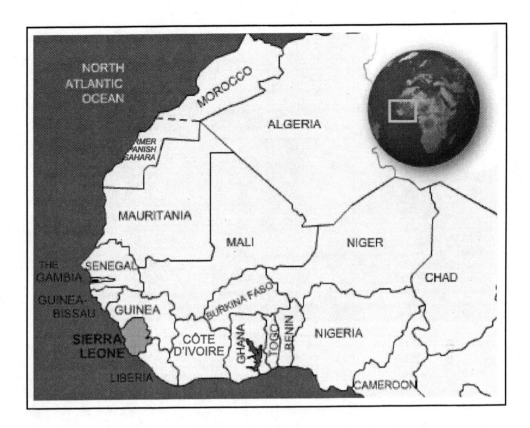

The area where the Bumbuna dam is located had also been deeply affected by the war. The dam became a strategic target for rebel forces during the conflict and witnessed two major battles fought around its premises. These battles led to the near complete destruction of the village of Bumbuna and to extensive human losses in the nearby communities. The dam site itself was attacked several times but never seized by the rebel troops.[2]

Within one year of the war's end, Sierra Leone's economy was already progressing,[3] although it was estimated that more than 80 percent of the population were still living below the poverty line of US$1 per day. It would take time for the country to recover from more than ten years of terrible civil war that had provoked the disruption of economic activities, the destruction of physical and social infrastructure, and the displacement of almost half of the population. The country's electricity infrastructure, primarily based on thermal generation with imported oil, had suffered from widespread destruction and lack of maintenance. Sparse coverage, unreliable electricity supply, and high electricity tariffs resulted.

The western area grid, including Freetown, was supplied from the Kingtom thermal generating station, which was in poor condition and extremely polluting. With aging equipment, it was capable of meeting less than 5 percent of the estimated power demand. As a result, a rotation system was established that supplied electricity to Freetown customers for only a few hours every three to seven days. Most towns in the interior of the country were largely or entirely without power supply, exacerbating the economic and social recovery.

---

2. The dam site was defended by mercenary troops paid by the contractor.
3. GDP growth rate had reached 6.5 percent in 2003.

UNAMSIL Helicopter used by the project staff to reach the project area.

The power supply situation was detrimental to the quality of life of Sierra Leonean citizens, to the development of small business, and to the competitiveness of the national industry. The population after dusk had the choice to remain in darkness, use candlelight or, for those with sufficient means, to run expensive, noisy and polluting generators.

Because of this situation, the efforts to complete the Bumbuna project apparently benefited from a wide consensus among Sierra Leoneans. The large majority of citizens placed high hopes on the project, which would finally supply the much-needed electricity to the capital, Freetown and other important towns suffering from severe power shortages.

However misinformation, skepticism and suspicion were alive in the Sierra Leone society, undermining confidence in the government's capacity to complete the project. Moreover, a tribal conflict between communities in the project area was stirring up opposition to the project. In this situation, the World Bank had to decide whether to participate together with the Government of Italy, the African Development Bank and other donors in financing the project.[4]

The World Bank considered:

- the sufficient guarantees of stability provided by the political situation and by the presence of UN forces;
- the financial and economic merits of completion of the project (which were high given that the dam and a considerable portion of the physical infrastructure were already been built);

---

4. In addition to contributing to the financing of the project, the role of the World Bank would have been to: i) catalyze private sector financing through an IDA "Partial Risk Guarantee" (PRG), and ii) ensure the application of sound environmental and social safeguards.

- the compliance with safeguard policies;
- the huge potential benefits that completion of the project offered for Sierra Leone's citizens and economy, and its role in contributing to stability;
- the role that the World Bank could play through its participation to catalyze private sector participation in completion of the project and enhancing the sustainability dimensions;
- apparent public support for the project throughout Sierra Leone's society.

and eventually decided to participate in this venture, with Board approval in June 2005.

Box 2. Messages Posted on a BBC e-forum on the Power Situation in Sierra Leone

Nearly every night of my entire 17 years of educational life has been spent studying by candlelight. And I know that it will remain so until I complete my degree course.

Studying with candles makes my course much harder and expensive, as I am always having to buy more candles. Sometimes I find it difficult to understand what I am studying—I often have to strain my eyes to see what is written in the books. The occasions when I have had electrical light do not compare—having a clear picture of what is written in the books makes me feel very happy while I study.

Foday Conteh, 27, student

Freetown is becoming a graveyard at night.

Sylvester Sahr Kapindi, Sierra Leone

It is disgraceful to say that it is over three good months now I can't see a light from our NPA. What troubles me most is when I get home from work; I can't have a rest at night at all. For every door you step through there must be a generator with different sounds, and when more than four of them Tiger generators start, the whole compound is full of noise

Shamo, Freetown

Currently, I'm running my business in an extremely difficult situation, as I am not making a profit because I have to spend so much cash generating power for my business. As there is virtually no power and electric light in Freetown It costs me a lot of money to use the generator, as I have to buy five gallons of fuel each day. The cost of fuel rises often. I can't increase my customer charges because if I do they will stop using my services. And so I a m running at a loss . . .

Feyi J Asgill, 37, owner of an internet business

How can we talk about attracting investment if we expect investors to generate their own electricity!? It is no coincidence that the symbol of ideas is a light bulb

Abi from Freetown

CHAPTER 2

The Communication-based Assessment (CBA)

Although disagreements over hydropower and other infrastructure development originates from various social, economic, and political causes, it has become increasingly apparent that it emerges or is exacerbated due to: different levels of understanding and perceptions of the actors involved; mistrust in the management of the decisionmaking process; lack of information; and lack of effective participation by key stakeholders—in particular the communities and people directly affected by the project. These controversies are not specific to infrastructure development projects, and often simply reflect the process in which given groups and societies express their opinions and come to decisions about development priorities.

Methodological Approach

It is essential to establish a communication component at the very beginning of the project cycle. In fact, any development project that regards people as mere recipients, rather than the actual creators or partners, of change and progress, is likely to fail. The social, cultural, and political aspects of a major hydropower project rival its technical challenges (Cunningham 2004).

The first step taken by the World Bank communication team in the BHP was to conduct the *Communication-based Assessment*. This assessment of the situation adopts communication techniques and tools to identify problems that must be addressed to ensure that: i) project development objectives are properly identified, understood and agreed to by the stakeholders, and ii) project implementation can proceed in a fair and efficient way, which ensures the achievement of project objectives.

The communication-based assessment identifies the political, social, and cultural environment of the project, and assesses the position of project stakeholders in terms of their respective:

- level of information;
- perceptions and concerns;

- attitudes;
- practices and behaviors; and
- interests.

The needs assessment was thus important to understand and anticipate: i) potential roadblocks, ii) the audiences to be reached, and iii) effective channels of communication. Finally, it explored the government's willingness and capacity to engage in two-way communication both through government channels and through the agencies responsible for the BHP project implementation. Underlying aims were to reduce or minimize the risk of controversy and threats to the project's successful completion, and building public support for the project by taking into account different stakeholder interests.

For Bumbuna, the communication team carried out the needs assessment by organizing over 30 in-depth interviews and consultations with selected players, including ministry officials, Members of Parliament, local government authorities, traditional tribal authorities, religious groups, civil society associations, universities, other development agencies, local and national media, communication professionals in Sierra Leone, as well as a direct sampling of project affected people at the site, and residents of Freetown.

Another important task in the initial phase was to *assess the media environment of Sierra Leone.* This included identifying existing media outlets, assessing their capacity to reach the different audiences, and evaluating their ethics and the professional quality and skills of the journalists.

An assessment of local NGOs was also completed to appraise their capacity to act as potential partners in the design and implementation of communication activities.

The communication-based assessment included an *assessment of the existing communication capacity* within the institutions involved in the project implementation. It also assessed the political willingness and commitment to communicate. To ensure the ownership of the communication process, each step in its design was taken with the national implementing institution that will eventually manage and assume responsibility for project communication activities.

Box 3. Tasks of the Communication-based Assessment

1) Understanding the history of the project.
2) Evaluating the political, social and cultural environment around the project.
3) Identifying stakeholders and assessing their level of information, perceptions, interests and concerns.
4) Identifying communication problems to be addressed and related objectives.
5) Assessing the government counterpart communication capacity.
6) Analyzing the available media (mass and proximity media) and communication professionals.
7) Designing a communication strategy and creating the conditions for its successful implementation.

The assessment of the institutional capacity to communicate is essential to identify deficits and prepare training modules and/or a technical assistance strategy tailored to local needs. Capacity building is always on the agenda of the World Bank's Development Communication Division (DevCom) and is the best way to ensure the sustainability of its intervention and the enhancement of local ownership of the project results.

Because the BHP involved the completion of an existing infrastructure, it was important to *retrace the history,* main events, prevailing circumstances and prior level of stakeholder involvement, starting from the project identification in the early 1970s. This effort helped to better gauge the perceptions and concerns of Sierra Leone's citizens in relation to this very symbolic, nationally relevant, and politically charged infrastructure project. Part of this information was gathered by the communication team and part was derived from an ex-post evaluation of stakeholder involvement in options assessment carried out in parallel with the communication planning work, as part of the EIA process.

Finally, *public opinion research* was commissioned and carried out by an independent consultant to assess the overall public perception concerning specifically:

(i)   the level of knowledge, the perceptions and the image of the BHP among the stakeholders and the public at large;

(ii) the communication needs and preferred channels;

(iii) the concerns related to social management issues such as the resettlement process (along the transmission line and Bumbuna reservoir area);

(iv) the key players involved and their respective roles; and

(v)   the expected deliverables of the project and related concerns.

The public opinion research was based on: i) a questionnaire submitted to a sample of 840 citizens of Freetown (including its rural districts) and of the main cities along the transmission line (Makeni, Port Loko and Lunsar); ii) nine focus group discussions (six with persons running small enterprises in Freetown, two with civil society organizations in Freetown and in Makeni and one with NPA[5] employees; and iii) 16 in depth interviews with large businesses, media houses/journalists, civil society organizations, and local authorities.

This study thus provided the baseline data against which monitoring and evaluation of the impact of communication activities are going to be measured.

Main Findings

In 2003, when DevCom was invited to be part of the Bumbuna Hydroelectric Project Team, the project was described as "benign," with limited adverse social and environmental impacts, and likely support from the public—in other words, manageable reputational risks and manageable project risks, primarily because the main construction risk was already absorbed.

However, once the communication team started working on the ground, a number of sensitive challenges emerged. The BHP, with its highly symbolic value, had raised many hopes and provoked significant disappointments and frustration in its three-decade history.[6] On one hand, it was the most important infrastructure project in the history of Sierra Leone, and a potential source of national pride.[7] On the other hand, it was a symbol of inefficiency,

---

5. National Power Authority, the national agency responsible for the production and distribution of electricity in Sierra Leone.

6. A significant example of these hopes and frustration is found in the website of the "Jus gi we di light" (just give us the light) campaign (www.jus-gi-we-di-light.info).

7. The dam is depicted in the 5000 leones bill, the largest denomination banknote in Sierra Leone.

corruption, and foreign exploitation, given the inability of a series of governments, over more than three decades, to complete a project so vital for the country—this despite project financing being available from donors. The citizens of the country therefore looked at the latest effort to complete the Bumbuna Hydroelectric Project with a mixture of hope, skepticism and unfulfilled expectation.

In addition, the communication assessment found that, since 1997, misinformation, rumors, and mistrust had been spreading among various groups of stakeholders nationwide, including among the communities living in the project area. Moreover, a thorny tribal conflict was taking place in the project area, which could frustrate and jeopardize all attempts to effectively involve local communities in the project design and implementation. There was also a risk that disagreements over project issues would aggravate local tensions. This was of particular importance as there were many tensions simmering below the surface within communities and among communities in the post-war situation.

The assessment thus demonstrated the urgent need to bridge information gaps, seek trustworthy dialog with the stakeholders, restore confidence, and enhance support for the completion of Bumbuna Hydro. To achieve these objectives, the project communication team started a comprehensive communication process.

From the beginning, it appeared that the communication team would face several difficulties. The project is located in a very poor, remote area. Many villages were difficult to access, and were reachable only after many hours or even days by foot, on mountainous terrain. In the more remote areas, visitors were so seldom seen, that villagers hid themselves in the bushes until they were convinced that the "strangers" had good intentions for coming into their vicinity. Second, several ethnic groups live near the project area and are affected by it, requiring the use of several different languages for communication activities.

Villagers near the project area.

The findings of the communication-based analysis are presented in more detail below. The first challenge related to the perceptions and concerns, and the level of information and participation of the project stakeholders. A communication strategy was prepared to address them. The second challenge concerned the institutional capacity to efficiently and effectively implement this communication strategy.

The main findings of the communication-based assessment are presented in more detail below. The first types of problem described are those related to the perceptions, concerns and level of information and participation of the project stakeholders. A communication strategy was prepared to address these. The second types of problem were those related to the institutional capacity to efficiently and effectively implement this communication strategy.

Main Problems to be Addressed by Communication Activities

Lack of Confidence. Sierra Leone has just emerged from a long and brutal civil war, and Sierra Leoneans are relieved, but still distrustful about their future. Concerning the project, the population was generally aware of the potential benefits of Bumbuna Hydro, and had great expectations. Its completion was seen by many as crucial for Sierra Leone. However, confidence in the actual completion of the project was lacking. This mistrust revolved around two main factors.

First, Sierra Leoneans were disillusioned about the neverending story of Bumbuna and the many struggles that had occurred since the beginning of the project. After 30 years of struggles, the citizens grew accustomed to Bumbuna only through its illustration on the 5000 Leone bank note. However, nothing concrete ever came from it, and Sierra Leone is still almost entirely without power. Bumbuna was becoming a joke. "When Bumbuna is completed" became a popular phrase, which indicated, "never."

Another factor was widespread mistrust of "corrupt politicians."[8] Because of its long and controversial history, Bumbuna Hydro was held up as an example of mismanagement, corruption, and the government's failure to deliver on its promises. This mistrust was common among the general public, as well as the project-affected people, who feared that the compen-

---

8. in 2004 one of the most popular singers in Sierra Leone released an album whose title was "we are fed up with corruption" that became a bestseller.

Box 4: Level of Information and Confidence in the BHP among Sierra Leone Citizens

The public opinion research confirmed that Bumbuna Hydro was widely known by Sierra Leone's citizens, as shown in the following table.

Have you heard about the Bumbuna Hydro?

Yes	92 %
No	8 %

Respondents were convinced of the potential benefits of the project . . .

Will the Bumbuna Hydro improve the situation in your area?

Yes	96 %
No	4 %

. . . but were lacking confidence in its actual completion.:

Do you have doubts about the actual completion of the BHP?

Yes	68 %
No	32 %

Source: BHP public opinion research

sation they were entitled to and promised, would be stolen. Unfortunately, there were grounds for this mistrust. In recent years, compensation promised for land confiscated for road constructions evaporated before reaching the intended recipients. Moreover, in the previous phases of the BHP, when the dam and its related quarry were built, the local communities were not consulted, and remained uncompensated for land lost.

Misinformation and Confusion about Roles. The general public, and especially the communities living in the project area, were confused about Bumbuna Hydro, whether it would resume or not, and when. Even high-ranking government officials exhibited misperceptions and lack of information about the project status.[9] The lack of information was particularly obvious concerning the roles of the different actors involved in the project. In the project area for instance, the Italian constructor of the dam, Salini Costruttori (locally called Salcost) was considered to be the only actor. In previous times, the constructor was left alone to establish and manage relationships with the local communities in the project area for the purpose of good-neighborliness. Also, urged by politicians in Freetown, Salcost made "presents" to local communities, but with two negative effects.[10] First, this developed a paternalist relationship between the contractor and local communities, which were begging the constructor instead of asking for their rights, of which they were not even fully aware. Second, it created a misperception that Salcost was the "owner" of the BHP, and that the government had no responsibilities toward the affected communities.

Rumors. Several misleading rumors related to the BHP were circulating among the general public and the local communities, embedded in a complete lack of adequate information at all levels in society. One of the most common rumors depicted Bumbuna as an example of foreign exploitation. Many believed that the Italian contractors (Salcost), with the agreement of some corrupt members of the government, would have voluntarily delayed the completion of the dam to be able to mine the site and smuggle gold and diamonds out of

---

9. During an interview, the Clerk of Parliament said the completion of Bumbuna Hydro was progressing at full speed and that all the cables and wiring along the transmission line from Freetown to the power plant were in place. In reality, over 20 towers of the transmission line had been destroyed by looters.

10. This is not a criticism of the contractor, but rather an observation that the contractor was made to play a role for which it was not suited.

Bumbuna hydroelectric power plant—work in progress.

the country.[11] Others felt that mismanagement of funds was the main issue, and that money allocated for social projects had been diverted to other, unrelated or fraudulent uses.

In interviews, the chief editor of a leading newspaper in Freetown observed that disillusionment due to widespread corruption and lack of adequate information had led to negative perceptions about the use of public funds for Bumbuna Hydro.

Community Conflict. Two main communities directly impacted by the project construction live in the Chiefdom where the dam was built: the *Donsogoia,* which belong to the *Koranko* ethnic group, and the *Kalanthuba,* which are *Limbas.* When the project preparation work for completion of BHP started, these two communities were locked in an intense tribal conflict over ruling power. The Paramount chief, a Donsogoian, was not recognized by the other community, which boycotted the chieftancy election of 2003. Since then, the elected chief had not been able to assert his authority in the Limba area, which incidentally, constitutes 70 percent of the chiefdom.

The Kalanthuba elders were therefore boycotting all activities of the Paramount Chief, including the consultations held with the BHP management, thus preventing the majority

---

11. This allegation could be easily proven wrong by visiting the dam site and studying its geological characteristics. The site sits on an area of granite where there are no diamonds, and along the shores of the river where little mining occurs, and where no mining would be possible without being seen by the surrounding populations.

A school near the project site.

of the population from expressing their concerns, opinions, and needs. This local struggle was about to be elevated to the national level by a "bill of rights" written by a local NGO from the Kalanthuba community. The bill was presented to the Parliament and national media to protest the "reckless" construction of the dam and "the lack of inclusion of the affected communities in the decisionmaking."

High Expectations of Local Communities. The project design originally anticipated monetary compensation only for those people directly affected by the project—those households that were going to suffer from loss or damage to structures and other properties, access to roads and other public services, access to natural resources (including forests and the river), crops and farmland, and all other losses associated with income-generating activities. During visits, over thirty years, political authorities made many promises and created many expectations among local communities, the most recurrent one being free electricity (when in fact the initial phases of the BHP project did not include significant rural electrification, except for Bumbuna Town). Public consultations clearly showed that local communities expected significant benefits from the huge investment project they were hosting.

The consultations carried out during this phase, and the timely overlap of the communication work with the broader social and environmental assessment, were instrumental to including a community development program for the whole catchment area in the project design.[12]

Problems Related to Communication Capacity

Government Capacity to Communicate. The capacity of the Government of Sierra Leone to communicate was determined to be extremely limited. The information on development

12. "Upper Seli Community Development Program."

was perceived as being incomplete, project-driven, and restricted to the President's and the government's political agenda.[13] The overall level of credibility of public news was considered low. A majority of people did not trust the sporadic information provided by government because of the many broken promises of the past, and inflated official statements about the progress of projects.

There seemed to be a chasm between the leading policy makers and the population at large, especially the poorest and most remote rural communities. A 2003 social assessment noted that, "an apparent disconnection between the perceptions of rural people and the government on agrarian issues is exacerbated by the failure of Parliamentarians to spend much time with rural constituencies" (Vincent 2003).

Minimization of the Role of Communication by Project Team. The minimization of the role of communication is a common problem in development projects that involve large physical construction activities. The role of communication is typically emphasized until it comes to allocating a budget. In particular, the national counterparts, which are usually bodies of the public administration, are unwilling to allocate significant funds to activities that are aimed at making their work more transparent and at enhancing the participation of a larger number of stakeholders.

In a pure, top-down approach, the role of communication is often seen as merely public relations and as a way to inform target groups about decisions made.

Limited Local Professional Capacity in Communication. As in many other post-conflict countries, it is difficult to find local capacity after years of civil war. Most of the skilled Sierra Leoneans have left the country, and those remaining are distributed among international development agencies and NGOs. This is especially true regarding local communication professionals, which generally see their function confined to the role of public relation officers, complying with the minimum expectations of national and, too often, international project managers.

Weak Media Environment. Both the print and broadcast media in Sierra Leone are weak and in need of basic training for journalists, technical support and better infrastructure. The assessment concluded that with some exceptions, journalists lacked a sense of civic responsibility and consciousness regarding professional ethics. It suggested that journalism is not investigative, and journalists do not play their essential role as members of the "fourth estate." Sensationalism prevails over objectivism, and a profusion of inexperienced newspaper reporters and editors are quickly yielding to the temptation to accept payments from people who want articles written to their specifications. The overall conclusion was that newspapers failed to tackle national issues from an analytical point of view, and were unable to explain the problems.

"There is a lot of recklessness" said Radio Democracy's leading newscaster. "Corruption in the country is not only rampant among the political elite of the society but also in the press." The stories carried by the most important newspapers and the national broadcast channels are closely related to the governmental agenda and its key subjects, but rarely cover the issues related to the needs of the population.

---

13. In early 2004, one of the highest government representatives announced on the radio that the works for the completion of the BHP had already started and that the project would be completed and fully functional before the end of the year. In reality, project funds were still not available and the completion of the project was expected to be by the end of 2006.

Low Capacity and Representation of Local NGOs. The capacity and representation of national NGOs in Sierra Leone is generally still fairly limited. Many among the national NGOs rely on assistance from foreign partner organizations. The assessment concluded that the overall perception of NGOs is negative and characterized by a broad lack of trust among pockets of the population. During the first consultations, the Bumbuna community clearly expressed their preference to interact directly with the project management and not through a third party, such as an NGO. In the aftermath of the war, many opportunistic organizations had quickly mobilized to profit from the initial inflows of foreign aid. Some of these acted as brokers between the communities and the donors, leading to numerous alleged cases of unequal treatment and fraud.

CHAPTER 3

Communication for Operational Support

The Strategy

The design of the communication intervention had to respond to the need for an open, transparent, and inclusive decisionmaking process, one that reflected stakeholders' concerns. It needed to help the government design an environmentally sustainable, socially equitable, and economically viable project.

To this end, a Communication Action Plan (CAP) was designed to establish a two-way communication mechanism and a continuous consultation process, allowing the government and the donors to actively and positively interact with all stakeholders.

The CAP was designed as a flexible tool, ready to be adapted according to the feedback received and the changing situation on the ground. The uncertainties related to working in a post-conflict scenario favored an approach in which the design of the communication strategy, instead of being entirely fixed at the outset, could be revised as communication activities progressed, and new knowledge and experience were gained. In such situations, the CAP is carried out through "monthly working plans" which take into account the long-term strategy as well as the immediate needs.

The Communication Action Plan (CAP)

In development, a communication strategy is defined as a comprehensive set of coherent communication activities aimed at achieving a project's communication objectives.

Graph 1. Communication Approach

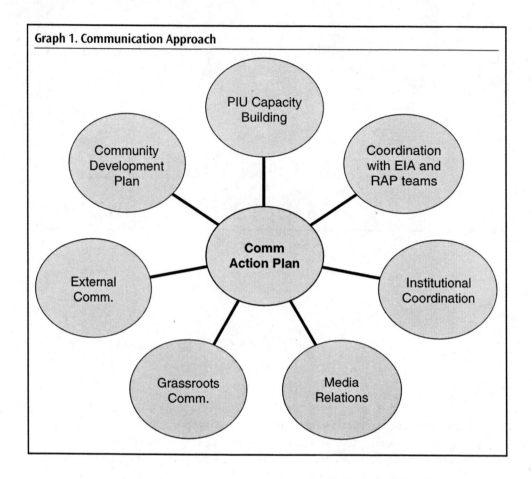

A communication objective is an objective[14] that requires some changes in the:

- level of information,
- perceptions,
- attitudes (intentions),
- practices and/or behaviors,
- level of participation, and/or
- level of empowerment

of specific groups of people, or an improvement in the level of:

- mutual understanding,
- cultural, social or knowledge exchange, and/or
- cooperation

between specific groups of people.

The definition above clearly demonstrates that most objectives of development projects (whether implicitly or explicitly) are or encompass communication objectives.

---

14. A project objective can be defined as a desired future situation that we want to reach through the implementation of project activities.

The communication objectives of the BHP were defined on the basis of the desired outcomes, risk reduction, and the communication deficits that were identified through the communication-based analysis. Given that the subject of a communication objective is always one or more groups of people defined as primary stakeholders or primary audiences,[15] the CAP has been subdivided into several components, each one directed to a specific audience/stakeholder group. In fact, several public, private, and international players are involved in the completion of the project, each one playing a different role and having different tasks and responsibilities at different levels (political, economic, and technical); characterized by different communication needs, problems and objectives; and requiring different strategies and media to be reached.

Box 5. Budget per Component Allocated for the CAP Implementation (US Dollars)	
Functioning of the Communication Unit	70,000
– *salaries*	*48,000*
– *training*	*2,500*
– *equipment*	*14,500*
– *running costs*	*5,000*
Communication with involved institutions	5,000
Communication with the general public	50,000
Communication with the local communities	50,000
Communication with the international community	7,000
monitoring and evaluation	18,000
TOTAL	**200,000**

The CBA showed that the main audiences that needed to be reached and the main stakeholders that needed to be engaged by the communication strategy were:

a) institutions involved in the project implementation such as donors, government institutions, contractors, and so forth;
b) general public (mainly through mass media); and
c) people living in the project area, including the project-affected people.

Given the concern of international NGOs about large infrastructure projects, and the related reputational risk for the World Bank and other financing partners, the international community was identified as a fourth audience.

In the following chapters, we introduce the main elements of the CAP.

Strengthening Local Capacity for Communication

Developing the local capacity to design and implement a communication strategy requires significant efforts in terms of technical and human resources. For the sake of sustainability, it is important to think about how the created capacity can produce benefits after the project completion. In general, it is preferable to create the capacity inside the beneficiary institution. In this case, however, the entity that would manage the generation and transmission facilities had not yet been established. Therefore, it was decided to establish a Communication Unit (CU) within the Project Implementation Unit (PIU), which is the executing body of the project, with the expectation of possible integration within the future hydropower management structure.

---

15. Often wrongly defined as "target groups." This term reveals the dated, top-down approach to communication in which groups are viewed as the passive receivers of a predefined message.

The PIU Communication Unit was created to:

(i) design and carry out all communication activities related to Bumbuna Hydropower Project;

(ii) act as a focal point and source of information for all stakeholders;

(iii) encourage exchange and collaboration between project staff members and stakeholders;

As previously mentioned, the local capacity in communication was very weak, and it was difficult to find local specialists who were both suitable and available. It was decided to recruit a person with an extensive knowledge of the project and the proven capacity to interact with local communities. The specialist's gaps in knowledge and experience were covered through technical assistance and support from DevCom as well as through some training courses on communication. An agreement was also signed with the "Information, Education and Communication Unit" of the "National Commission for Social Action" (NACSA), a separate World Bank-financed project, to provide technical assistance and quality control for the Bumbuna Hydro communication activities. NaCSA in fact had already developed experience in development communication that was unique in Sierra Leone.

Despite DevCom and NaCSA-IEC support, the effort to build technical communication capacity within the PIU was not sufficient to produce the expected results. Project managers in fact are often jealous of the information they possess, and have the tendency to retain that information. Moreover, they frequently put the project communication activities under their tight control. This situation can frustrate, and even compromise efforts to provide adequate communication support, and can lead to a complete stall of the communication activities.

To avoid this problem and create ownership of the communication function, it was necessary to create consensus on the communication strategy and plan among the PIU managers and the Bumbuna Technical Committee, which is the inter-ministerial supervising body of the PIU. This consensus required extensive efforts and was possible only with the direct involvement of both bodies in the

---

Box 6. Roles and Responsibilities in the Management Structure of the BHP

A *Minister Cabinet Subcommittee* is responsible for all issues related to policy decisions concerning the Bumbuna Hydroelectric Project. The Subcommittee is chaired by the Vice President and is composed of the Minister of Energy and Power, the Minister of Finance, the Minister of Development and Economic Planning, the Minister of Lands, Housing, Country Planning and Environment and the Minister of Works;

A *Technical Committee* addresses the technical aspects of the project and reports to the Cabinet Sub-committee for directives. The Technical Committee comprises high-level officials of the concerned ministries and other institutions.

A *Project Implementation Unit (PIU)* is the executing body of the project. It directly manages the project budget and ensures the proper and timely implementation of all project activities. The PIU selects and appoints consultants to carry out specific studies or works and ensure the liaison with all stakeholders and donors. The PIU reports directly to the Technical Committee;

The completion of the construction of the dam and of the powerhouse is being carried out by *Salini Costruttori* (otherwise known as Salcost), while the completion of the construction of the transmission line is carried out by *ABB Italia*. The Italian engineering firm *Studio Pietrangeli* is responsible for the supervision of works.

monthly planning of the communication activities. These monthly meetings allowed them to contribute to the design and approve the "monthly working plan." Despite this, the PIU did not confer the necessary autonomy to the CU in the management of funds allocated to communication activities. As a result, on many occasions, the responsiveness of the CU was undermined, and planned communication activities delayed.

Another important step was to establish the practice by which the communication officer would participate in all-important meetings, including the technical ones. The terms of reference for the communication officer specified that he/she would be the focal point for all project information. The participation of the CU in project activities stimulates the continuous interaction with the project managers, which is essential to any responsible and successful communication program.

Communicating with the Institutions Involved in the Project

At the beginning of the new completion phase, general confusion about the Bumbuna Hydro progress was evident among government institutions. The lack of information during project negotiations with donors triggered various rumors and speculation fueled by short-term political interests. During a World Bank project preparation mission, the team learned that one of the highest government representatives had publicly announced that work on Bumbuna Hydro was nearly complete, contrary to the reality on the ground. On a similar occasion, another high-ranking official declared that the project was being delayed because of "unreasonable donor conditions." This misinformation was then relayed by the press, which was providing incorrect, incoherent, and unverified information on the project.

It was therefore urgent to prepare communication activities to address this situation by ensuring that all institutions involved in the project implementation:

- had a common understanding of the project objectives and strategy,
- shared the same information and knowledge by being regularly informed about relevant facts and decisions, and
- had the opportunity to express their views, opinions and proposals on the different issues concerning the project.

This would allow each of these institutions and the project team experts working in the various sectors of the project, (social, environmental, economic, engineering) to feel part of the initiative and be motivated to provide valuable input to it. It also allowed them to disseminate objective and uniform information whenever they were in contact with other stakeholders or with the press.

Given the relatively small number of these audiences, and the relatively easy access to them, the activities selected to achieve these objectives were:

- face-to-face and group meetings,
- organization of workshops involving different stakeholders on strategic communication or other relevant issues,
- production of written briefs distributed to all involved institutions, and
- production of a Bumbuna Hydro newsletter.

Communicating with the General Public

The general public of Freetown, the western area grid, and the main towns[16] along the transmission line were considered to be major stakeholders of Bumbuna Hydropower Project. As electricity consumers they were direct beneficiaries of the project output.

The communication objectives directed to the general public were:

- to provide correct information about the progress of the BHP, its expected benefits, and the role of the different organizations involved (government, donors, contractors);
- to gather feedback and suggestions from the general public for consideration by decisionmakers; and
- to identify and address specific information gaps and erroneous beliefs concerning the project.

The media environment analysis identified radio as the most effective mass media channel to reach the general public. This was confirmed by the public opinion research study. As shown in the opposite box, the people place the greatest trust in information provided by the radio.

This component of the CAP has been subdivided into two modules. The first component is tailored to journalists and media outlets as an intermediate audience and interpreters of public opinion. This module seeks to stimulate journalists to talk about the Bumbuna Hydro and to ensure that they possess valid and reliable information on which to build their articles and news reports. The second component aims at reaching the general public directly by producing, broadcasts and disseminating communication products such as TV/radio programs and printed material.

It is important to stress that mass media activities (in particular radio programs) and activities for the journalists were aimed not only at informing and sensitizing audiences, but also at developing mechanisms for the CU to gather feedback from the audiences.[17] The CU regularly integrates the results of this process into the Communication Action Plan.

Module 1. Regular Interaction with Journalists of the Print and Electronic Media

This module consisted of nurturing direct relationships and dialog with journalists and providing them with material they could use when producing articles and news reports. Once this relation is established, journalists can be key partners in helping the CU reach all segments of civil society.

The activities within this module were designed to:

- establish a telephone and email contact point for the mass media and for other interested people and organizations;
- prepare and regularly update a journalist and media directory and select the most relevant and interested journalists and media outlets;

---

16. Port Loko, Lunsar, and Makeni.

17. This was achieved primarily through radio phone-in programs in which citizens would call the program and interact with the panelist live.

Box 7. Results of Public Opinion Research on Sources of Information

From which source did you first hear about the BHP?

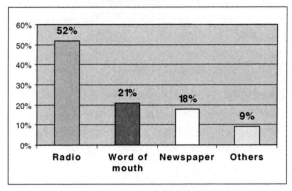

How do you usually get information?

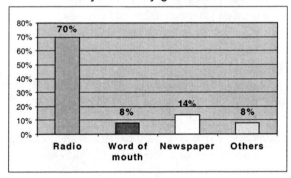

What is the source of information you trust the most?

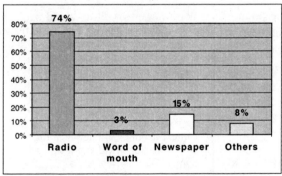

The low score given to "word of mouth" can be explained by the sample audience, which was composed pimarily of urban residents.

- regularly issue press releases;
- produce and update an information package (press kits) for journalists, with informational material, pictures, interviews (written and on tape), and so forth;
- monitor relevant mass media output;
- organize press conferences for important events; and
- organize visits for journalists to Bumbuna to allow them to see the work progress.

Module 2. Production of Communication Tools

Radio is a very powerful medium in Sierra Leone. Most people (even in the most remote areas) have radio receivers, are regular listeners, and are accustomed to participating in phone-in programs. Radio is therefore one of the best ways to engage in dialog with the public.

This module focused on the production of radio programs in different formats:

- Phone-in programs: very successful in Sierra Leone, these programs consist of discussions between speakers in the studio and the public calling from home to express their opinions and ask questions.
- News reports: produced whenever there is the need to disseminate specific information to the population, broadcast by national and local radio.
- Panel discussions: bringing together different stakeholders to discuss specific issues concerning the project.
- Radio theatre: radio plays produced to describe the Bumbuna Hydro and its benefits, and to address people's concerns identified through feedback mechanisms.

Some television programs have also been produced. These can have a high impact, although on a very limited audience, as few households have television sets and the required power generators. The households that can afford it, often subscribe to a re-broadcasting service and therefore watch foreign channels. The reach of television has been typically considered as limited to affluent citizens of Freetown.

Finally, this module included the production of printed material such as:

- project leaflets,
- project brochure, and
- billboards to be placed in strategic settings in Freetown and in Makeni.

> **Box 8. Presenting the World Bank and its Role**
>
> The involvement of the World Bank and other international donors is a factor of trust for the public opinion and for the PAP. In a context of perceived widespread corruption it can raise confidence among the local population that the project will be carried out properly. It is therefore useful to publicize the role and involvement of the World Bank in the project while stressing the leadership role of the government and the responsibilities of the local authorities and citizens. It is essential in a post-war context to build confidence in the capacity of the country and of its citizens to stand up and take their own development on themselves.
>
> It was important on one hand to highlight the fact that the Bumbuna Hydro was managed by the Sierra Leone government, and on the other hand that the World Bank and the other donors were acting not only as financial contributor but also as a guarantee for a transparent, inclusive and fair project.

Communicating with the Local Communities

The previous phases of the BHP left a negative local legacy. Local communities in the reservoir area had not been adequately informed of the project impacts and the implications on their environment, and lives, and were only marginally consulted or involved in project preparation and implementation. Moreover, households and communities whose lands were appropriated for the quarry and building site never received the promised compensation. The result was a widespread discontent and suspicion toward government officials and all other project staff visiting the area.

The first task of the CU was to build trust and credibility among project area residents who had been left with years of uncertainty and were afraid that their villages and fields would be submerged. This task could only be achieved by establishing a direct relationship with the community and demonstrating responsiveness to their concerns.

At the start of the communication work, BHP project staff approached local communities through traditional chiefs and elders, an established procedure in Sierra Leone, and held public consultations in the most accessible villages. Consultations were aimed at informing the communities about the progress of Bumbuna Hydro, gathering feedback, discussing concerns and introducing the CU. Despite the remoteness of many communities along the reservoirs, the use of traditional communication methods (town-crier sent out by traditional authorities) ensured that representatives from all hamlets in the region could attend the consultations. This traditional communication method proved to be one of the most effective ways of disseminating information and stimulating participation

Public meeting in the village of Kafogo.

among the local communities. Thanks to the use of this well-accepted process, the communities felt reassured and became aware of the existence of a contact point in the Bumbuna Hydro Management (the CU) that they could reach and rely upon whenever they needed information, wanted to express concerns or identify a problem.

The process helped to achieve the objective of establishing a two-way relationship to:

- provide local communities with timely information on the project, its impacts, its timing, its progress, and so forth, and
- allow them to express their concerns and grievances and ensure that these are properly taken into account in the decisionmaking process.

Regular interactions with local authorities and visits of staff of the Communication Unit to the concerned communities were complemented by radio programs in different languages broadcast on local radio. An assessment of radio programs received and listened to in the different villages allowed the CU to identify which radio stations and which languages to use when disseminating information.

As the Communication-based Analysis showed, the most urgent information gap to be addressed concerned the status of implementation of the BHP and the expected impacts of the resulting reservoir on villages and fields. The communities also needed to be reassured that the filling of the reservoir would begin after the completion of the resettlement and compensation process.

Another important issue to clarify was the role of the different actors involved in the project. As previously mentioned, in the past, local communities understood the constructor to be their only project counterpart. In contrast, in this new phase, the leading role and responsibilities of the government had to be emphasized. The role of the World Bank also had to be explained. The local communities saw World Bank involvement as an important guarantee, not only for the completion of the project, but also for a fair resettlement and compensation process. This trust in the World Bank became even stronger due to the intermediary role that the DevCom and CU staff played in the tribal conflict that led to the organization of a "peace and reconciliation workshop."

Finally, it was felt that the communication component of the BHP could do more than just build a bridge between the project and the local communities. It could also help the local commu-

---

Box 9: Relationship Between the CU and the Other Project Teams

Collaboration between the Communication Unit and other project teams (including other project experts, donors and government officials) visiting the area is essential to ensure coherence of the information and to facilitate the interaction with the local communities. This is particularly true in the project preparation phase, when the Environment Impact Assessment (EIA) and the Resettlement Action Plan (RAP) are prepared with the involvement of the local communities.

On the other hand the CU can benefit from the extensive visits and studies that the EIA and RAP teams carry out in the project area. In the case of Bumbuna Hydro for instance, the RAP team disseminated key information agreed with the CU. The RAP team also provided the CU with a precise picture of the cultural, social and economic context as well as an accurate assessment of the communities' concerns. This information was extremely valuable for the CU to design follow-up communication activities.

nities to break their long isolation and create a venue to discuss and plan their own development. The idea of setting up a Bumbuna community radio station was discussed with the local communities and, after their endorsement, included in the CAP.

A community radio station is a key tool to foster dialog on new development initiatives. This is even more important in a context where local communities are facing important changes in their environment. They will have to adapt to and learn how to benefit from the new opportunities offered by the reservoir (fishing, transportation, and even tourism) or by the new supply of electricity to the village of Bumbuna. A community radio station is also an ideal medium to develop a sense of community identity and cohesion, and a vehicle for dialog and local civic participation, which is extremely important in a post-conflict context.

The radio, called Radio Numbara, 102.5 FM, has been set up with the support of Radio Netherlands, which provided equipment and technical and managerial training. It is important to note that the community radio is not a "project radio," but is fully owned and managed by the community, which has appointed a management board composed of representatives of both genders of all social and ethnic groups. The community will adopt programming formats and contents that respond to development objectives and community service requirements as established by community members themselves. The community radio is also a useful medium of the Bumbuna Hydro Communication Unit to disseminate information about the project and promote the participation of local communities in project activities.

Communicating with the International Community

This component focused on making information concerning Bumbuna Hydro available to international audiences (development agencies, international NGOs, academia, the Sierra Leone diaspora, and so forth). In the development and academic world, there is a widespread interest in new methodologies to develop large infrastructure projects and, in particular, in dealing with their environmental and social impacts.

For these reasons, a project website[18] was designed and launched as a knowledge-sharing tool. This website contains information on the project, on its context and on its expected impacts and benefits. It also includes a comprehensive "Question and Answer" section and allows downloading of project documents and reports. Through the contacts provided in the website, any interested person can request additional information or provide feedback.

The website was also designed to ensure transparency of the project financing and decisionmaking process. This recognizes that the development community, especially advocacy organizations active in the social and environmental sector, monitors all large infrastructure projects, and organizes campaigns against specific projects. The CAP considered it important to ensure that these institutions had access to all of the information they required to demonstrate transparency, adherence to safeguards procedures; and the positive impact of the project on the development and living conditions in Sierra Leone.

---

18. www.bumbuna.com

Boys in the village of Kakeko.

The website is also publicized in Sierra Leone; however, the Internet is still beyond the reach of the vast majority of the population.

First Results of the Communication Work

This case study was written at the beginning of the project implementation phase. However, despite a very modest budget, some grassroots and mass communication activities had already been carried out with positive results. During project preparation, in fact, the communication-based assessment was instrumental not only to setting the stage for future communication work, but also to beginning interaction with the different stakeholders.

Local Communities Confident and Cooperative

While there is no quantitative evidence at this stage, it can be reasonably concluded that the communities living in the project area now have access to and possess the basic information they require on the status of the Bumbuna project and how it impacts them. The rumors and mistrust have been neutralized, and exaggerated expectations mitigated.[19] The multiple visits, information and consultation sessions by the CU and the other project teams, created the ground for the establishment of a climate of trust between the project management and the local communities. Today, local communities know to whom they can refer whenever they need information or want to express concerns or grievances.

---

19. Many within the project affected communities were convinced that the resumption of works would imply the employment of large numbers of local residents. In reality the employment needs pertained to highly technical expertise, entirely lacking in the area, and only a few locals could have been hired for unskilled labour such as maintenance of premises, cleaning of the reservoir before inundations, etc.

Community Conflict Solved

The community conflict that existed in the Chiefdom where the dam is located was based on a disputed chieftancy election. While this conflict was unrelated to the project, it could have undermined it by jeopardizing the smooth completion of the consultation process due to protests and boycotts of project works.

The CU adopted a proactive approach to mitigate this risk. After a series of contacts with the representatives of the two communities, it facilitated a local "peace and reconciliation workshop," which was attended by more than 300 representatives of all 105 villages and towns of the chiefdom, including elders, section and villages chiefs, women and youth leaders. This community workshop paved the way for reconciliation between the two ethnic groups. It also strengthened the dialog and built trust between the BHP project and the community, as demonstrated by the following quotes from the workshop report written by one of the participants:[20]

> . . . what the government failed to achieve in 2 years 7 months, the indigenes, victims of injustice and the World Bank (the BHP Project Communications Unit supported by the project preparation works) have achieved in 2 days. This clearly depicts the effectiveness of the bottom up and participatory approach in conflict resolution and development.
>
> The peace achieved in Bumbuna is a sure sign that the people are ready for development. The project contractors and authorities will now have the opportunity of working in a peaceful atmosphere . . .

Lack of Opposition to the Dam Project

Many dam projects, including those supported by the World Bank, are the object of national and international scrutiny and hostile campaigns. In the case of Bumbuna, no sign of opposition is detectable at national and international levels. This is, among others factors, a consequence of the dialog established with national NGOs, the early involvement of local stakeholders, and the meaningful consultation process, which created legitimacy.

Communication Included in the Project Design

Since the beginning of the project completion phase, the communication work gained recognition and was considered one of the analytical underpinnings of the project design. The communication work was reflected in all the project preparatory documents including the Project Appraisal Document, the legally binding Development Grant Agreement and the Project Implementation Plan.

The Website as a Useful Interactive Tool

The project website[21] proved to be a very interactive tool with external audiences. Its use surpassed the initial expectations as it attracted different types of net users such as professionals, students, politicians and the media. The website was used for different purposes,

---

20. Thomas Moore-Turay July 30th 2005.
21. www.bumbuna.com

such as requests for information, requests for material for documentary production and news stories, student thesis preparation, and e-forum discussions.

Involvement of Sierra Leone's Diaspora

An unexpected result of the communication activities was a resulting strong interest in the Bumbuna Hydropower project among the Sierra Leone diaspora in Europe and in the USA. In fact, they represent the large majority of the website visitors and of over 200 newsletter subscribers to date. From the interaction established with some of them, it appears that the donors' pledge to complete the Bumbuna project has helped to break a negative psychological spell among the Sierra Leone diaspora, which is now finally starting to believe in the country's ability to recover. The result is that they have begun re-engaging and investing their energy, skills and financial resources in their home country.

As a model, the communication process has led to the birth of several initiatives and proposals by Sierra Leonean professionals who are starting collective actions to promote business opportunities in Sierra Leone. An example is the "Sierra Leone is open for business" initiative, a truly spontaneous effort leading to a planned 2006 Sierra Leone Energy and Private Sector Development Conference.

Notwithstanding the achieved results, much more could be obtained were it not for the recurring delays caused by a shortage in funds.

CHAPTER 4

Lessons Learned

The experience of communication in the BHP is an ongoing story, yet it has yielded some lessons, which may prove applicable to other infrastructure projects.

Understanding the Context

Retrace the History of the Infrastructure Project

Infrastructure projects typically have a long and intricate history. The identification and design phases can extend over many years, followed by lengthy construction works. Whenever a project involves the completion or rehabilitation/safety of an already existing infrastructure, it is important to retrace the history of the project, from a technical, economical, political, social, and environmental point of view. This helps to explain the reasons for the choices that have been made and to immediately identify any possible negative legacies of the project. Social and environmental aspects did not have the same weight in the past as today. It is particularly essential to verify whether the different stakeholders were involved in the first phase of the project and if the affected people were properly identified and compensated.

Identify Stakeholders and Assess Their Perceptions

As with all interventions, it is necessary to have a clear knowledge and understanding of the social, cultural, and economic context of the project. This analysis must include the identification and assessment of the project stakeholders, their power structure, the interest groups they represent, how they perceive the project risks and ways to mitigate those risks, their perception of the distribution of costs and benefits, their communication channels and any existing conflicts among them.

It is then important to assess stakeholders' concerns, expectations, interests, and perceptions of project-related risks, based on which they will support or oppose a project.[22] This assessment should also be extended to cover the mass media (what do they know about the project?), relevant representatives of the public administration (are they committed?) as well as local and national authorities (is there a political struggle among them or in relation to the project?).

Finally, the assessment should include the stakeholders' perceptions in relation to the different organizations involved in the project financing and implementation. As in the case of Bumbuna Hydro, this should also lead to the identification of erroneous beliefs and rumors, which in some cases can be devastating if not addressed in a timely fashion.

Involving the Stakeholders in Project Design

Start Consulting Stakeholders from the Beginning of Project Identification

The identification phase of large infrastructure projects is usually long. The local populations that are likely to be affected by the project are usually informed and consulted during the Environmental Impact Assessment (EIA) and Resettlement Action Plans (RAPs), which are often carried out near the end of this phase.[23] In the meantime, the concerns and expectations of project affected people and the other stakeholders grow, and they begin to demand to be kept informed and to be able to express their point of view. Moreover, designing the project taking into consideration from the beginning the opinions and proposals of the stakeholders can reduce the project preparation costs by limiting the risk of future objections and conflicts, which may lead to costly adjustments and/or delays.

Therefore, a two-way communication process must be moved upstream in the planning process and must be integrated in the project design. Involving stakeholders in the design process creates legitimacy, local ownership and, as a consequence, sustainability.

Establish or Strengthen Credibility with Local Communities

Through coherence. Local communities may receive visits for different reasons by government bodies, donors, NGOs, and expert teams. Local communities will ask questions indiscriminately to these visitors about the project, its progress, its impacts and possible compensation. It is important to avoid contradictions on these issues. Some field missions may provide uninformed answers, which hamper the trust and credibility that have been built with the communities and, in some cases, provoke undue alarm or over-expectations. It is impor-

---

22. Often concerns are justified by what happened in the previous phases. For instance, during the first phases of the dam construction, the PAP were not compensated, and therefore they were very concerned about the completion of the project, which would involve the flooding of the area behind the dam with loss of fields and in some cases of homes.

23. A better approach is the use of the "Strategic Environmental Assessment" with appropriate stakeholder involvement.

tant to brief the different field missions and share all information about the project and about the relations with the local communities. When possible, the communication officer should accompany all local missions.

Through responsiveness. Consultations are costly to the local communities. To attend them they must interrupt their activities and duties and sometimes they must travel long distances. For this reason local communities must see that their participation is meaningful. Their questions must receive answers, their doubts and concerns must be addressed, and promises must be kept. Otherwise confidence and cooperation will be lost.

Support the Local Communities in Identifying Their Needs

Usually, large infrastructure projects benefit the urban population more than the communities (typically rural) living in the project area. However, the new practice favors the development of mutually beneficial mechanisms for local communities through complementary development projects financed by revenue sharing. Communication activities must support the local communities in discussing and identifying their priority needs and outlining a strategy to fulfill them. To this end, a community radio station can be extremely effective.

Communication in Project Implementation

Entrust Autonomy to the Communication Unit

While the planning of the communication activities must be prepared in close collaboration with the project management and the other technical teams, the CU must have autonomy in the implementation of the activities as well as in the day-to-day work. This implies that the CU must have direct access to the budget allocated to communication activities following periodic working plan agreements. This mechanism will prevent possible blockages of communication activities by project managers wishing to control the implementation of these activities without having the necessary time and skills.

Organize Information to be Released Officially

Specific activities must be devised to ensure that all officially released information is correct and coherent. This can be done by: i) creating a common understanding among the project staff on the role of communication; ii) producing printed material (such as a newsletter) to provide updated information to the project staff and other interested people; iii) coordinating media interventions; and iv) identifying and training key staff to become active spokespersons and communication "champions."

Ensure Transparency

Nothing sows the seeds of mistrust more than the feeling that something is being kept secret. "Facts rarely inflict any lasting damage even if unpopular or bad news."[24]

---

24. Raymond E. Cunningham, CAL Energy international, ltd.

Truthfulness, transparency, and participation are the best way to avoid criticism. This has to be achieved in a proactive way, disseminating information and project documents. Websites are the most cost-effective media.

. . . and Don't Forget the Project Staff

Internal communication within the project team is essential for the smooth and efficient implementation of the project. To be motivated and able to efficiently accomplish its own tasks, each project staff member and partner must understand and share the mission, objectives, and strategy of the project. She/he must be fully aware of his or her role and responsibilities, the actions she/he has to undertake, the procedures she/he has to follow and how to react to events.

This can be achieved by:

- Creating mechanisms and occasions (group meetings, workshops) allowing all staff members to express their own views, opinions, and proposals on the different issues concerning strategies and actions.
- Guaranteeing the accessibility/availability to the project staff and partners of data, information and procedures instrumental to the understanding and to the proper implementation of everyone's tasks.
- Providing the management at the different levels with all information necessary to make the most appropriate decisions, facilitating a smooth communication flow from the decentralized offices to headquarters can save time and resources.

CHAPTER 5

Conclusions

M ost of the lessons learned from Bumbuna Hydro seem logical—even obvious. However, implementing them requires experience, time, and budget. In most cases, the government counterpart and the project team leader agree on the principles and objectives of the communication strategy. Yet, when it comes to allocating a specific budget, communication is not a priority . . . unless there are obviously high political and reputational risks associated with the project, which result in attempts to deliver propaganda to gain support. However, development projects don't need to be advertized and "sold." Propaganda can even be counter-productive. Transparency and participation are the best way to avoid criticism and opposition.

Communication applied to development initiatives is still too often limited to activities aimed at informing the stakeholders or the general public following the typical and dated top-down approach. Government counterparts and project managers are often not used or ready to "democratize" the decisionmaking process, but are more interested in accelerating it.

However, the budget, time and effort devoted to communication will almost certainly be worthwhile. The Bumbuna Hydro experience shows that setting up a two-way communication process from the beginning of the project cycle is crucial to:

- design a project that is responsive to real needs;
- ensure local ownership and sustainability of the project; and
- avoid future problems and criticisms, which may delay and even stop the project at a later stage.

A recent study (World Bank 2004) commissioned by the World Bank, in partnership with Hydro Quebec analyzed 16 large hydropower projects and found out that the main factors in project failure were directly or indirectly related to communication.[25] Nearly all participants in this study brought up early involvement of local communities and potentially affected populations in the project planning as key to its successful implementation:

> Even if the public participation process may add time and costs to a project, this is nothing compared to the cost of canceling a project or of struggling on for several years . . .
>
> The balance of past experience is clearly in favor of finding ways to associate the public in project planning and design, especially with respect to the planning and design of project-related environmental and social mitigation and compensation requirements.

The cumulative experience of decades of infrastructure projects, which have been widely discussed and evaluated, demonstrate that stakeholder involvement and horizontal communication are no longer an option but an obligation. To comply with this new development paradigm, every future infrastructure project should, from its inception, include communication as an analytical tool as well as a key ingredient for project design and implementation.

---

25. Such as: lack of awareness of affected people, lack of recognition of affected people'e representatives, local communities not well organized to defend their rights, lack of community involvement from the start, lack of consultation program and poor communication process, lack of NGO pressure.

Bibliography

Cunningham, Raymond E. 2004. *Managing the Social Aspects of Major Projects.* Hydro Vision 2004, HCI Publications 4 (www.hcipub.com).

Danaiya Usher, Ann. 1997. *Dams as Aid: A Political Anatomy of Nordic Development Thinking.* Routledge Studies in Development and Society.

Dubash, Navroz K., Mairi Dupar, Smitu Kothari, and Tundu Lissu. 2001. *A Watershed in Global Governance? An Independent Assessment of the World Commission on Dams.*

Dreze, Jean, Meera Samson, and Satyajit Singh. 1997. *The Dam & the Nation: Displacement and Resettlement in the Narmada Valley.* Delhi: Oxford University Press.

IUCN. 1997. *Large Dams: Learning From the Past Looking at the Future.*

McCully, Patrick. 1996. *Silenced Rivers: The Ecology and Politics of Large Dams.* Zed Books.

Singh, Shekhar and Pranab Banerji. 2002. *Large Dams in India, Environmental, Social & Economic Impacts.* Indian Institute of Public Administration.

UNDP. 2005. *Human Development Report.*

Vincent, James. 2003. *The Social Assessment Study.* Freetown.

World Bank. 2003a. *World Bank Water Resource Sector Strategy, 2003.*

——. 2003b. "World Bank Infrastructure Action Plan." Informal Board Meeting, July 8th.

——. 2003c. "Stakeholder Involvement in Options Assessment: Promoting Dialogue in Meeting Water and Energy Needs. A Sourcebook." ESMAP Report, ESM264, July.

——. 2004. "Quality Management of Safeguards in Dam Projects." Unpublished paper by HydroQuebec International for World Bank, December.

———. 2005a. "Communications in Infrastructure Projects: World Bank Experience and Lessons Learned." Unpublished paper, Development Communication Division, The World Bank.

———. 2005b. *World Development Indicators.*

World Commission on Dams. 2000. "Dams and Development. A new framework for decision-making. The WCD Report."

BHP project documents[26]:

Project Appraisal Document (PAD).
Environmental Impact Assessment (EIA).
Resettlement Action Plan for the Reservoir and Dam Area.
Upper Seli River Community Development Initiative (USCDI).

---

26. Available in the BHP website (www.bumbuna.com).